The Boy Who Started
C E L T I C

THIS is the story of a boy, a calf and one of the biggest football clubs in the world.

It is also a story of how one person can change many people's lives.

All great journeys begin with a single step. As a boy, Brother Walfrid did not know he was starting a great journey when he sold a calf at County Sligo's Ballymote Fair and took the boat to Scotland.

Every day, people are starting great journeys and they don't even know it. They are just trying, like Walfrid, to make people's lives better by helping others who are not as lucky as them. Walfrid helped people and started one of the world's most well-known football clubs.

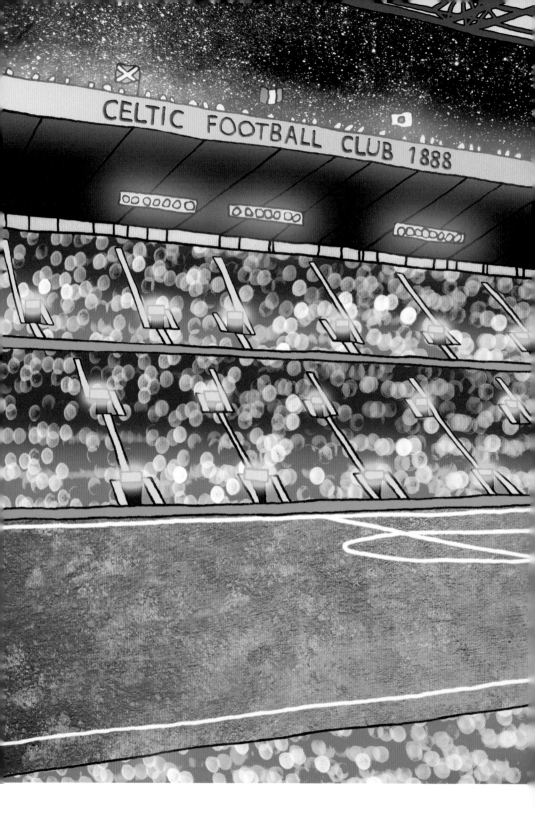

The Boy Who Started CELTIC

ALISON HEALY

with PAUL FRANCIS WILKIE

ARGYLL ✧ PUBLISHING

First published by
Argyll Publishing
an imprint of Thirsty Books
www.thirstybooks.com

British Library Cataloguing-in-Publication Data.
A catalogue record for this book in available from the
British Library.

ISBN 978 1 7399922 8 6

Acknowledgement is made to Sonya Leonard and the Tom Leonard
Literary Estate for the use of the poem 'Fireaworks' on page 53.

Typeset & design: derek.rodger21@outlook.com
Illustration: www.PaulFrancisWilkie.com
Printing: Bell & Bain Ltd, Glasgow

In memory of my mother Mary Kerins, who
was Brother Walfrid's grand niece
AH

and to
Ivar Francis Wilkie
PFW

This map shows the way from Sligo to Glasgow that Andrew took as a boy. The towns in Scotland are where many Irish people went to find work.

1. Sligo
2. Greenock
3. Port Glasgow
4. Dumbarton
5. Paisley
6. Glasgow
7. Coatbridge
8. Hamilton
9. Edinburgh
10. Dundee

CONTENTS

1
The Boy and the Calf

THIS is the story of a boy, a calf and one of the biggest football clubs in the world.

It is also a story of how one person can change people's lives. But none of this would have happened without the calf. So, let's go back to the beginning.

The story of Glasgow Celtic began when Andrew Kerins was born in 1840. He was from a small farm in Ballymote, County Sligo, in the north west of Ireland.

When Andrew was five years old, the people of Ireland faced a huge disaster. Their potato crops died.

Andrew Kerins' early life on a small farm in Ireland when the potato crop fails and people starve.

You might wonder why that was a disaster. Could they not eat pasta instead? Or rice? Or pizza? Well, in 1845, many Irish people ate potatoes for all their meals. Especially if they were poor.

So, it was a very, very bad thing when their potato crops got a disease called blight and died. They had nothing else to eat.

The Irish Famine lasted for four years and about one million people died from hunger and disease during this time. Almost two million people left the country to find a better life in places like America, Canada, England and Scotland.

Some people died on their way to these countries. It was one of the worst things to ever happen in Ireland.

What can they do? Catch a boat to Scotland?

2
Off to Glasgow

ANDREW was lucky to survive the Famine but he knew that the small farm would not be able to feed everyone in his family. He would have to leave Ireland. It cost a lot of money to go to America because it was so far away, but England and Scotland were easier to get to.

Some people travelled to Glasgow on a boat from Sligo town. But where would he get the money for his fare? He was only 15 years old. Andrew Kerins and his friend, Bart McGettrick, decided to sell a calf at Ballymote Fair. This raised enough money to pay for their journey to Scotland.

Andrew sells a calf to raise money to travel to Scotland.

They sailed out of Sligo on a coal boat in 1855. Can you imagine what it was like for the boy from a small Irish farm to arrive in the city of Glasgow? He thought Sligo town was a very big place but Glasgow had more than ten times as many people living there. He had never seen so many people in the same place.

Thousands of Irish people had come to Glasgow before Andrew, so he heard Irish accents everywhere. But it was not easy for Irish people to find jobs and places to live. Many of them lived in very poor and overcrowded rooms. The unlucky ones caught diseases and became very sick.

On the boat to Glasgow

Luck was still on Andrew's side. He started work in the railway yard at Springburn. We don't know a lot more about his life at this time, because it was so long ago. But records show that after work each day he started taking night classes at a local school.

It is not easy for Irish people to find jobs and places to live in Glasgow. Andrew finds a job labouring on the railway.

Some of the teachers in this school were Marist brothers. The Marist order is a Catholic religious group that works with people in need. This inspired Andrew to work as a pupil teacher. Then, when he was 24, he made a very important decision. He travelled to France to become a Marist brother.

When Andrew came back to Glasgow, he had a new name: Brother Walfrid. Everyone who became a Marist Brother was given a new name. Andrew got this unusual new name because he was named after an Italian saint, Galfrido, who was called Saint Walfrid in France.

Andrew decides to become a Marist Brother and he later returns to Glasgow as Brother Walfrid.

He taught in London for a short time and then returned to Glasgow where he began teaching in a Marist junior school in the Calton, in the east end of the city.

Children going to Catholic schools had to pay a small fee at that time. He noticed that children were not coming to school because their parents could not afford to pay. It was only a few pennies but some people had to make the choice between eating, and sending their children to school.

Off to Glasgow

Glasgow becomes a big city in the 1800s

3
Feeding the Hungry Children

BROTHER Walfrid really wanted to help these poor hungry children. He thought long and hard about ways he might help.

Walfrid was a teacher in Saint Mary's school in the Calton and he set up an after-school club to help pupils with their reading outside school. And he asked people with shops and offices to give jobs to the children when they left school.

He noticed that the children had so much fun playing football, so he started a football league. 'If it gives then a reason to come to school, then I am happy,' he thought.

Brother Walfrid at the Sacred Heart school thinks about the Marist Brothers' mission to help people in need.

He was becoming a leader in the community and this was noticed. Soon, he was made headmaster of a new school nearby in Bridgeton, called the Sacred Heart Primary School. You won't be surprised to hear that he set up a football team in the new school.

Lots of people knew that the children were hungry but why do you think Brother Walfrid wanted to do something about it?

Was it because he came from Ireland, where people had suffered so much during the Famine?

Or was it because of his strong religious faith that taught him to help others?

Or was he just one of those people who always try to fix problems?

Brother Walfrid helps hungry and poor children through his penny dinner scheme at the school.

Perhaps it was a mixture of all those things that made him want to help people who were hungry or who needed education or a place to live.

'We must fix this,' he decided. His friend, another Marist, Brother Dorotheus, was working as a teacher in his old school, Saint Mary's. Dorotheus also saw the hunger in the children's eyes.

'We must fix this,' Brother Dorotheus said. Brother Walfrid asked the Society of Saint Vincent de Paul if it would help him to start a penny dinner scheme at local schools. Saint Vincent de Paul is a Christian charity that helps people who do not have enough money for food, heat and other important things.

The charity agreed to help. It was decided that children would pay one penny and they would get a good nourishing dinner at school every day. Even if they did not have one penny, the school would still feed them.

This was a great idea. Brother Dorotheus started the first penny dinner scheme at his school and it worked so well that Brother Walfrid's school brought in the scheme one year later.

It made Brother Walfrid and Brother Dorotheus happy to know that the children got at least one good hot meal every day.

Brother Walfrid starts a football league and
reading club at his school in the Calton.

4
Raising money and starting Celtic

BUT all these dinners cost money and many poor people were asking the Saint Vincent de Paul society for help at that time.

Brother Walfrid and Brother Dorotheus noticed that football was becoming very popular. Some people were paying money to watch matches.

An Edinburgh team called Hibernians had many fans in Glasgow so, in 1886 Brother Walfrid asked the Hibernians team to come to Glasgow to play a charity match against Clyde FC. More than 1,000 (one thousand) people came and paid to watch the match. This raised lots of money to pay for school dinners.

Another charity match was organised and this was even better – more than 15,000 (fifteen thousand) people came. Brother Walfrid was delighted.

Then he had an even better idea: Why not start a football club and charge people to watch the matches? This would mean that there would always be money to make dinners for children in need. And it would mean that Saint Vincent de Paul could spend its money on helping more poor people.

Brother Walfrid is made headmaster of a new school in Bridgeton and starts a football team.

Brother Dorotheus worked with him on the plan. After a meeting on November 6th, 1887, it was announced that Glasgow Celtic Football Club had been set up.

'A football club will be formed,' he said on that day, 'for the maintenance of dinner tables for the children and unemployed.'

Some people thought the club should be called Glasgow Hibernians but Brother Walfrid said he preferred the name Glasgow Celtic. He liked the way it linked Scotland and Ireland because they were both Celtic countries.

Brother Walfrid starts Glasgow Celtic Football Club.
He stands in front of Celtic's first badge.

The new team played its first match against Glasgow Rangers on May 28th, 1888. Almost 2,000 (two thousand) people watched Celtic beat Rangers by five goals to two. The teams would become each other's biggest rivals.

It was a good start for Celtic and it got even better the following year when Celtic reached the Scottish Cup Final. But more importantly, the new club raised more than £400 for local charities in its first year. That was a lot of money in 1888 and it would do a lot of good things for people in need.

Glasgow Celtic won the Scottish Cup Final in 1892 and moved into its bigger and better Celtic Park the same year.

5
Moving to London, then Dumfries

BROTHER Walfrid was so pleased that Celtic had won the Scottish Cup but 1892 was also a sad year for him because he was needed in London.

Glasgow had been his home for more than half his life and it must have been difficult for him to leave. Then, some time later, the Marist order wanted him to take over a school in Whitechapel, in the east end of London.

He quickly discovered that Whitechapel shared some problems with Glasgow. It had many poor and hungry people too. Brother Walfrid was getting older, but he was ready for the challenge.

He set up clubs in London for young men and boys and helped to provide free breakfasts for hungry people. Brother Walfrid did this work for ten years.

But he never forgot about the little football club he started in Glasgow and it must have made him very happy to see that it was growing all the time.

When his work was done in London, Brother Walfrid was needed at a Marist school in Kent. Finally, it was time to rest. He spent his last years in the Marist order's home, Saint Joseph's at Dumfries in Scotland.

Even after he retired, Walfrid used to keep up with the football results every Saturday. Of course he could not check the results on the television or the internet because this was so long ago. Instead, he asked friends to send the final score by telegram, which was an urgent message delivered by hand. He was delighted every time Celtic won.

Walfrid died on April 17th, 1915 just before he turned age 75. His beloved Celtic team won the Scottish League Championship on the same day. Walfrid lies at rest in the Marist burial ground at Saint Joseph's and his grave is still visited by Celtic supporters.

6
Celtic and Charity

A STATUE in memory of Brother Walfrid at Celtic Park keeps a watchful eye on the city he adopted as his home all those years ago. What would he think of the club he started? Do you think he would be proud?

Well, let's see. Today, Glasgow Celtic is one of the best-known football teams in the world. It was the first British club to win the European Cup in 1967. It has won the Scottish Cup Final, the Scottish League Championship and the Scottish League Cup more than 100 times.

It set up Scotland's first professional women's

football team in 2018 and has the biggest football stadium in Scotland.

It's difficult to put a figure on it, but it's thought there are more than nine million Celtic fans around the world. Fans have set up hundreds of supporters' clubs in at least thirty countries. Back in Ireland, Celtic is one of the most popular football teams. Isn't that incredible?

But probably most importantly for Brother Walfrid, Celtic has not forgotten about charity. The Celtic FC Foundation has raised more than £30 million for needy causes. They help people at home and abroad with food parcels, electricity bills, clean water projects and helping people to find jobs. The club still counts charity work as one of the most important things it does.

All great journeys begin with a single step. Brother Walfrid did not know he was starting a great journey when he sold that calf at Ballymote Fair and took the boat to Scotland.

He did not know he was taking a very important step in that journey when he joined the Marist order. And what a great step he took when he started Glasgow Celtic. Of course he did not know this was a great step. He was just trying to make sure that children had enough to eat when they came to school.

Every day, people around us are starting great journeys and we don't even know it. They don't even know it. They are just trying to make people's lives better by helping people who are not as lucky as them.

Perhaps you might start a great journey of your own some day?

THE END

Brother Walfrid's efforts had a lasting impact on the children in
his community and on the football club he founded.

Did you know?

- Glasgow Celtic has two mascots, Hoopy and Hailey, the huddle hounds. They love to meet young fans before matches at Celtic Park.

- Brother Walfrid always pronounced Celtic with a 'k', like Keltic.

- Celtic is famous for the green hoops on the jerseys, but the first club jerseys were white. Then they changed to green vertical stripes. The green hoops were first worn in 1903 and are still worn today.

- Celtic's first manager Willie Maley was in charge for 43 years. Wow! During this time, the club won 30 trophies.

- Glasgow Celtic has lots of famous fans, including singers Rod Stewart and Lewis Capaldi. And Celtic FC once shared a photo of Iron Man star Robert Downey Jnr wearing a Hoops jersey.

- Paradise is the nickname of the Celtic Park stadium. If you really love Celtic, you can have your wedding at Celtic Park. It would be a match made in Paradise.

- Footballers from around the world love to play for Celtic. Japan, India, the US and the Ivory Coast are just a few of the 50 or so countries represented on the Celtic team over the years.

- Celtic's all-time highest goal-scorer was Jimmy McGrory who scored an amazing 468 goals in major competitions in his long Celtic career. He was the club's highest scorer in every season except one between 1924 and 1937. He later became Celtic's manager for 20 years between 1945 and 1965. The second highest goal-scorer? Bobby Lennox in the 1960s and 70s with 273 goals.

- During World War I, Celtic Park hosted a women's football match between England and Scotland. In 1919, it was very unusual to see

Jimmy McGrory, Celtic's all-time highest scorer with 468 goals

women playing football and more than 15,000 people watched it. The organisers also had donkeys and an airplane display, to keep the supporters entertained. England won, 4-0.

• When the new Celtic Park stadium was built in 1892, a sod of grass was brought from Donegal in Ireland and placed in the middle of the pitch, to remember the Irish connection with the club. It was placed there by Irish man Michael Davitt, who fought for the rights of small, poor farmers to be treated fairly by landlords.

• Another sod of grass was brought over from Donegal in 1995 when the pitch was revamped. So there is always a small part of Celtic Park that is forever Irish.

• You don't expect to find an egg in a trophy cabinet but there is a very special egg at Celtic Park. It is a Fabergé egg, made from silver, enamel and yellow and black gold. The Fabergé jewellers were famous for making these very valuable eggs for the Tsars, who once ruled Russia. This egg was made for Jimmy Johnstone, once voted Celtic's all-time greatest player by fans. He had motor neurone disease and after Sarah Fabergé heard about his illness, she wanted to do something. She had 19 eggs made to raise funds to help him.

The precious Fabergé egg made in honour of the man voted by fans as Celtic's greatest-ever player, Jimmy Johnstone.

- Of the 11 players on the pitch when Celtic won the 1967 European Cup Final 2:1 against Inter Milan, 10 of them came from homes within 12 miles of Celtic Park. In other words, they were all locals. All except one – Bobby Lennox came from the Ayrshire town of Ardrossan 30 miles away.

- Liverpool and Celtic supporters have a lot in common, especially *You'll Never Walk Alone*, the song they sing before matches. The only question is, who sings it better?

- Many of Celtic's achievements have been written about in song and poetry and plays. Here is a poem called *Fireworks* written by the well-known Scottish poet Tom Leonard who was a big Celtic supporter. Tom felt strongly that the language people actually speak should be respected:

Fireworks

upcumzthi wee man
beats three men
slingsowra crackir

an Lennox
aw yi wahntia seenim
coolizza queue cumbir

bump

rightnthi riggin
poastij stamp
a rocket

that wuzzit
that wuzzthi end

finisht

The Boy Who Started Celtic

Sport Improving People's Lives

IT'S A LONG time since Brother Walfrid helped set up Celtic FC so that he could raise money to feed hungry people. The sad thing is that some people still do not have enough money to feed, and care for, their families. The good news is that there are lots of sports stars who want to help people who are not as lucky as them. . .

- You might know **Marcus Rashford**, the Manchester United player. His football skills made him famous but he uses his fame to help others. His family did not have a lot of money when he was growing up and he got free school meals. When Covid-19 closed schools in Britain, he was afraid that children would be hungry, so he delivered food to families who needed it. And then he got the Government to change its mind and give free school meals to children during the holidays.

  He also started a book club to give free books to children who need them. Doesn't he sound like a modern Brother Walfrid?

• **Serena Williams** is one of the greatest tennis players of all time. She uses her great wealth to make life easier for other people.

She helps Unicef – the United Nations' Children's Fund – which works with children who need help the most. After her sister was shot dead, she set up a centre in her name, to help people who have been affected by violence.

Like Marcus Rashford, she was worried about people being hungry during the Covid-19 pandemic so she gave more than 50,000 meals to families who needed them.

And when American schools opened up again during the pandemic she helped a company to give more than four million free face masks to children so that they could return to school safely.

- **LeBron James** is an American basketball player who never forgot his home town of Akron, Ohio.

He grew up poor and remembers there was so little food in the house that it could all fit on top of the fridge. He set up a foundation so he could help families from Akron in many ways.

He makes it easier for children to stay in school and he also funds after-school activities. He even pays for children to go to college. Once, he paid for 5,000 children and their families from Akron to go to an amusement park. Wouldn't it be great if every town had a LeBron James?

Walfrid's Wish Comes True

BROTHER Walfrid would be happy to see that his football club has not forgotten why it was set up.

Celtic FC Foundation is the club's charity. Its motto is 'Football for Good', and it raises money so that it can help people who need it the most. It helps people in Scotland, London, New York, Ireland, and in Africa.

These are some of the things it does:

- Gives people food and heating

- Helps people to get jobs

- Stops older people from feeling lonely

- Helps people to be fit and healthy

- Makes sure that all children are included, and that no one is left out

It has raised more than £30 million (almost €34 million) to do all this work. So Brother Walfrid's dream to help people is still coming true, more than one hundred years later.

Statues and Memorials

THIS STATUE of Brother Walfrid stands at the top of the Celtic Way, at the main entrance to Celtic Park. It was unveiled on 5th November 2005. Celtic supporters raised the money so that sculptor Kate Robinson could make the statue.

This memorial was built in Andrew Kerins' home town of Ballymote, County Sligo in 2004. It was paid for by money raised by ordinary people.

This is Brother Walfrid's simple gravestone at Saint Joseph's College in Dumfries. It is often covered with green and white Celtic scarves.

The Boy Who Started Celtic

Celtic Achievements

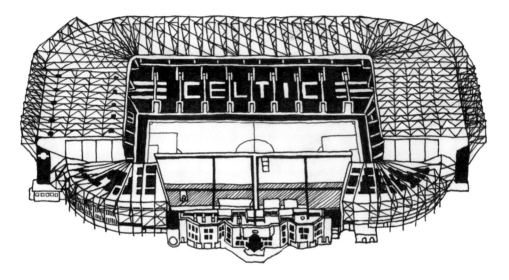

- At the time of writing in early 2023, Celtic have won:

  the **Scottish league championship** 52 times;

  the **Scottish Cup** 40 times;

  the **Scottish League Cup** 21 times;

  and the **European Cup** once.

  They have also been runners-up in the **European Cup Final** once (against Feyenoord in 1970) and were runners-up in the **UEFA Cup Final** once (against Porto in 2003).

- Celtic won nine league titles in a row, not once, but twice. They first did it in between 1965 and 1974, and again between 2011 and 2020.

- Like the men's team, Celtic FC's women's team got into winning ways quickly. They were set up in 2007 and reached the Scottish Women's Cup Final in their debut season. They won the Scottish Women's Premier League Cup in 2010 and 2021 and they also won the Scottish Women's Cup Final in 2022. What will they do next?

Acknowledgements

MANY PEOPLE helped me to turn Brother Walfrid's story into this book. They include Dr Michael Connolly who spent years studying Brother Walfrid's life. His book, *Walfrid, A Life of Faith, Community and Football* tells you everything you need to know about Brother Walfrid, and Glasgow Celtic's beginnings.

Thank you to Brother Brendan Geary from the Marist Brothers for your help. Thanks too, to the people of Ballymote who erected a monument to Brother Walfrid and named a park after him. Thanks especially to Ballymote Heritage Group and to Neal Farry for preserving his memory.

Thank you to Glasgow Celtic FC and to Tony Hamilton from Celtic FC Foundation for answering all my questions. Thanks too, to Paul Cuddihy and Joe Sullivan of the *Celtic View* magazine for all their help. And thanks to Sonya Leonard for allowing us to use her late husband's poem, *Fireworks*.

This book would not exist without the support of my publisher Derek Rodger, and without the illustrations from Paul Wilkie, so a huge thank you to you both. Thanks too, to all the Healys and Loughlins for your support.

Finally, thanks to all those Celtic supporters who have kept Brother Walfrid's memory alive and who support the club's charitable work.

Alison Healy
April 2023

About the author:

Alison Healy is an Irish writer from Ballymote, Co Sligo. There are many Celtic supporters in Ireland, and she remembers being very excited when she first heard she was related to Brother Walfrid. He was her mother's grand uncle.

Her first children's book *How Billy Brown Saved the Queen* was published by Little Island Books. She also writes articles for *The Irish Times*.

About the illustrator:

Paul Francis Wilkie is a Coatbridge-born, Celtic-supporting graduate of the Glasgow School of Art. www.PaulFrancisWilkie.com